The Nativity of (

MW01042655

Written by Lily Parascheva Rowe
Illustrated by Roland J. Ford

St. Stylianos Books

www.stylianosbooks.com
Copyright © 2010 St. Stylianos Books
1442 Dartmouth Avenue, Parkville, MD 21234
ISBN: 978-0-9831531-7-7

Second Edition

Scripture taken from the New King James Version.
Copyright 1982 by Thomas Nelson, Inc. Used by permission. All rights reserved.

The Feast of the Nativity of our Lord Jesus Christ on December 25 (Jan 7) is a very special day for Orthodox Christians. On this day, the Church offers a beautiful Liturgy in honor of Christ's birth. We remember that Christ was born of the Holy Spirit and Mary, the Theotokos.

Jesus' mother is Mary, the Theotokos. Jesus' Father is God. Jesus is the only person to ever have God as his Father. He is the only person who is fully God and fully Man.

This icon is called Virgin of Tenderness. You can see an icon like this one on the iconostasis of our Church.

It shows us that the baby Jesus is God himself, who became man. He did this so that we could know him.

This is the icon of the Nativity of Christ. It shows us the whole story of the birth of Jesus Christ.

Would you like to see what the different pictures in the icon mean, and hear the story of our Savior's birth?

Joseph was Mary's husband. Joseph was tempted to doubt that the baby inside Mary was really the Son of God. Joseph overcame this temptation. He became the Protector of our Lord Jesus and his blessed Mother.

When the baby was almost due, Mary and Joseph traveled to a city in Judea called Bethlehem. James, Joseph's son, went with them. They needed to be counted for a census. Mary rode on a donkey for the long journey.

Mary felt that she would give birth soon. Joseph tried to find a place for them to stay in Bethlehem, but the city was too crowded with other travelers.

They found a cave where animals were kept. There, they rested from their journey. Isaiah prophesied, "The ox knows his owner, and the donkey his master's crib," so it was right that an ox and donkey were present at their Creator's birth.

The cave was dark because of the darkness of sin in the world. Christ is the light of the world and illumines the dark places. This is why we sing, "Your Nativity, O Christ Our God, Has shown to the world the light of wisdom!"

While Mary was in the cave, she gave birth to baby Jesus, who is Christ our King and our God. She swaddled him in bands of cloth. There was no crib, so she lay him in a manger, a box for the animals' food.

We sing, "Today the Virgin gives birth to the Transcendent One, And the earth offers a cave to the Unapproachable One!"

The icon shows us two women who helped Mary by giving baby Jesus His first bath. This teaches us that like any other baby, He ate, slept, and needed to be bathed.

In a field nearby, shepherds were watching their flocks by night. An angel of the Lord appeared to them and said, "Do not be afraid, for behold, I bring you good tidings of great joy which will be to all people. For there is born to you this day, in the city of David, a Savior, who is Christ the Lord. And this will be the sign to you: You will find a Babe wrapped swaddling cloths, lying in a manger."

"Suddenly there were a multitude of angels saying "Glory to God in the highest, and on earth peace, goodwill toward men!"

It would be strange to find a baby in an animals' feed box! But the shepherds went to see, and found the baby Jesus, just as the angels had said. They told everyone what they had heard and seen, and all were amazed.

Far away, in the East, lived wise men who studied the stars because they wanted to know God. They saw a star in the sky as a sign that Christ had been born. We sing about this star. "For by it, those who worshiped the stars, were taught by a star to adore Thee, the Sun of Righteousness, and to know Thee, the Orient on high."

The wise men came to Jerusalem and asked the king of Israel, King Herod, "Where is He who has been born King of the Jews? For we have seen His star in the East and have come to worship Him".

Herod was afraid this new king would replace him. He did not understand that Jesus was not an earthly king, but a heavenly king. King Herod lied to the wise men and said that he wanted to worship Jesus too. He told them to go and find the baby, and then return to tell him where He was. Secretly, he wanted to destroy the child.

The wise men followed the star until they found Jesus. It took them a long time, and Jesus was a little boy by then. They found Him with His mother Mary, the Theotokos, at the house where they lived.

The wise men worshiped Jesus and brought him gifts of gold, frankincense, and myrrh. They show us that people all over the world would come to worship the Lord Jesus Christ.

While the wise men slept, they had a dream warning them not to return to Herod. They went home by a different way, so that Jesus would not be found and destroyed by the evil King Herod.

We sing "Angels with shepherds glorify Him! The wise men journey with a star! Since, for our sake, the Eternal God has been born as a Little Child!"

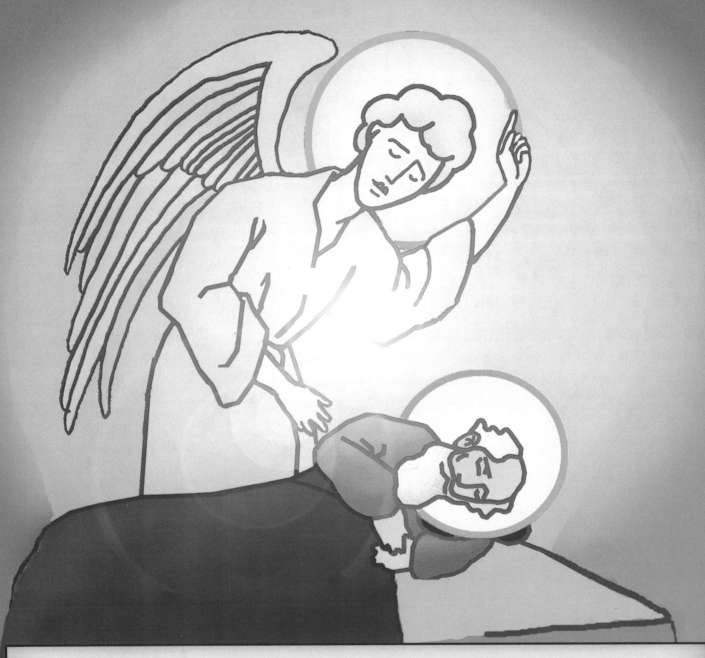

An angel of the Lord appeared to Joseph in a dream, and told him of King Herod's evil desires. The messenger of God told Joseph that he should take the Holy Family to Egypt and stay there until it was safe to return.

When Joseph awoke, he took Mary and her son to Egypt, just as the angel has instructed him to do. Joseph obeyed God and protected Christ Jesus and His mother from King Herod. They lived safely in Egypt until the evil king had died.

People all over the world celebrate Christmas. We decorate our homes, have parties, and exchange gifts. While we enjoy these things, we must remember that the true meaning of Christmas is in the birth of Jesus Christ. It is in this way that God, the Creator, was born a man. He saved us from sin and death by becoming one of us.

Troparion (Tone 4)

Your Nativity, O Christ our God,
Has shone to the world the Light of wisdom!
For by it, those who worshipped the stars,
Were taught by a Star to adore You,
The Sun of Righteousness,
And to know You, the Orient from on High.
O Lord, glory to You!

Kontakion (Tone 3)

Today the Virgin gives birth to the Transcendent One,
And the earth offers a cave to the Unapproachable One!
Angels with shepherds glorify Him!
The wise men journey with a star!
Since for our sake the Eternal God was born as a Little Child!

Dear Parents,

This book teaches children the story of the Nativity as celebrated in the Orthodox Church. Through repetition your child will learn to recognize the icon associated with the feast and understand the elements within the icon. Children will also learn to recognize certain phrases in the Liturgical celebration of the feast and how all of these Traditions tie together with the narrative of the story. We encourage you to refer back to the icon when reading this book to help younger children make this connection. It is our hope that this book and others produced by St. Stylianos Books will provide a useful tool to help parents educate children in the faith of the Orthodox Church.

St. Stylianos Books

St. Stylianos Books
Orthodox Children's Books
www.StylianosBooks.com

Printed in the USA
CPSIA information can be obtained
at www.ICGtesting.com
LVHW062221031223
765600LV00035B/272